CONTENTS

A world to protect

Imagine piling into the family car and driving for several hours, then stopping in a huge car park and joining an enormous queue.

Along with thousands of other people, you shuffle slowly forward and then, an hour or two later, round a bend and take out your digital camera to photograph the attraction shielded behind a clear plastic wall. Impatient people behind you force you forward and eventually

Landscapes such as this scorched Spanish countryside could become common around the world unless people take action to protect the environment.

Greenpeace

Sean Connolly

FRANKLIN WATTS
LONDON•SYDNEY

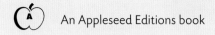
An Appleseed Editions book

First published in 2008 by Franklin Watts
338 Euston Road, London NW1 3BH

Franklin Watts Australia
Hachette Children's Books
Level 17/207 Kent St, Sydney, NSW 2000

© 2008 Appleseed Editions

Created by Appleseed Editions Ltd,
Well House, Friars Hill, Guestling,
East Sussex TN35 4ET

Designed by Helen James
Edited by Mary-Jane Wilkins
Picture research by Su Alexander

ISBN 978 07496 8073 2

Dewey Classification: 363.7

A CIP catalogue for this book is available from the British Library.

Photograph acknowledgements
page 6 Jose Fuste Raga/Corbis; 8 Rainer Hackenberg/Zefa/Corbis; 10 Bettmann/
Corbis; 11 Erik Schaffer; Ecoscene/Corbis; 13 Robert Keziere/Greenpeace;
14 Rex Weyler/Greenpeace; 15 Patrick Moore/Greenpeace; 17 & 18 Greenpeace;
20 Mark Avery/Orange County Register/Corbis; 22 Reuters/Corbis; 23 Marcos
Brindicci/Reuters/Corbis; 25 Greenpeace/Corbis/Sygma; 26 Paul Langrock/
Zenit/Greenpeace; 27 Daniel Beltra/Greenpeace; 28 Paul Langrock DE/
Greenpeace; 29 Miguel Angel Gremo/Greenpeace; 30 Greenpeace;
31 John Miller/Greenpeace; 33 Steve Morgan/Greenpeace; 35 Greenpeace;
37 Richard Sobol/Zuma/Corbis; 38 Salem Kreiger/Greenpeace USA;
39 courtesy Tetra Pak; 40 John Ishii/Greenpeace; 42 John Wilkinson/
Ecoscene/Corbis
Front cover Reuters/Corbis

Printed in Hong Kong

Franklin Watts is a division of Hachette Children's Books

back towards the car. Once you reach home again, you e-mail your friends photos of the attraction – an oak tree, protected in its own tiny nature reserve.

A bad dream?

This probably seems a strange nightmare – and perhaps that is all it will be. We will wake up to find not just one or two ancient trees near us, but billions all around the world. The air around us will be clear and clean, like the water in the streams, lakes and oceans. Animals will have space to live as they have for millions of years.

But this view of the world is beginning to seem as unreal as the nightmare. Many animals are threatened by humans, and many species are now extinct. Pollution is a problem, threatening the purity of both air and water, while poisons in the soil find their way into our food. Ancient forests are cut down and wetlands filled in and built on. In some ways, the nightmare view of the future is beginning to take shape.

Lasting efforts

This alarming view of the world is not new. People have been aware of the threat to the natural world for decades and activists campaign for change. The international organization Greenpeace is a leading campaigning group in the battle to protect the environment. It has warned about the real dangers for more than 35 years. Greenpeace has also taken action against these threats, and its members have risked (and in one case, lost) their lives for the cause.

ON THE SCENE ... ON THE SCENE

'When the last tree is cut down, the last river poisoned, and the last fish dead, we will discover that we can't eat money.'

Quote on a Greenpeace banner

Today Greenpeace is one of the best-known and most successful organizations within the environmental movement. It cooperates with others who share its aims, but is always prepared to lead the way as it fights to preserve the Earth's resources.

Seeds of protest

For thousands of years humans thought that the Earth's resources were limitless. Oceans and plains stretched beyond the horizon. Rivers and streams brought a constant flow of fresh water. Forests provided what seemed like an endless supply of wood for shelter and fuel.

If one part of the world became overcrowded or short of food, people could explore other regions. People from Asia found new lands to settle: Australia to the south, the Americas to the east and Europe to the west. In this spirit of exploration and discovery, Europeans later set up colonies in Africa, Asia, Australasia and North and South America. This process was under way in the eighteenth century, when the Industrial Revolution

Some of America's most dramatic countryside is protected in Grand Teton National Park in Wyoming. Since the late nineteenth century, governments have been pressed to set aside large areas of natural beauty

began in Europe. The changes which began with the Industrial Revolution brought many advances, but people began to realize that there would be a price to pay for this progress.

The price of progress

Humans themselves paid dearly for industrial progress. Huge mills and factories produced goods by the thousands, but the people who worked in them suffered. Workers were injured or killed in workplace accidents. Others developed serious illnesses related to working conditions – from handling or breathing in dangerous chemicals. The rapid development also had a negative effect on the Earth.

Although people in the 1800s would not have used the word, it was the environment that suffered as a result of the rush to build new factories and use new industrial methods. Great Britain became rich and successful because of the Industrial Revolution, but its countryside began to suffer. British forests were cut down for fuel, rivers became polluted with waste and cities were filled with foul-smelling fumes from chemical factories. These fumes mixed with fog to create what we now call smog: it was during this time that London was given the nickname the Smoke.

Most people felt that although these effects were unpleasant, they were unavoidable. Others, however, raised their voices in protest. The artist and poet William Blake wrote about satanic mills ruining the England he loved. Concern also grew in other countries that were changing as a result of the new industries. In 1866, the German scientist Ernst Heinrich Haeckel first used the word ecology to describe the relationship between plants and animals and their physical environment. Americans could see that their country – which they had once considered limitless – was also affected.

Founding Greenpeace

Bob Hunter was a journalist who became one of the founders of Greenpeace. Thirty years later he recalled: 'In Vancouver at that time there was a convergence of hippies, draft dodgers, Tibetan monks, seadogs, artists, radical ecologists, rebel journalists, Quakers and expatriate Yanks in the major city... closest to Amchitka Island, where the US wanted to explode a bomb. Greenpeace was born of all of this.'

Taking things forward

People in some parts of the world listened to the voices of environmental protest – at least to a degree. Countries set aside unspoiled land as reserves and natural parks. Some animals and plants were protected. But industry continued to develop, and the great wars of the twentieth century added to the natural destruction.

During the 1960s, a new generation of protesters found a voice. Some activists struggled to promote racial equality and civil rights. Others aimed to spread a message of peace, especially in war-torn Vietnam, where the United States had sent hundreds of thousands of soldiers. There were also protests about the damage to the environment caused by the rapidly changing world.

The Canadian city of Vancouver became a centre for many of these protests, which often overlapped, with anti-war protesters adding their voices to the those belonging to the environmental movement, and so on. Vancouver has a beautiful setting, with forested mountains rising up from the Pacific Ocean. Its inhabitants have always been proud of the unspoiled natural beauty of their city.

Above
These trees in Germany's Black Forest have been damaged by acid rain, caused when destructive waste chemicals from factories blend with rainwater.

Opposite
China exploded its first atomic bomb in 1964, making it the fifth world power (at that time) to possess nuclear weapons.

By the mid-1960s, another group had arrived in Vancouver – young Americans who crossed the border to Canada to avoid being sent to fight in the Vietnam War. Like their Canadian hosts, they had a keen love of nature and the environment. Meanwhile, the US had begun testing nuclear weapons under the Aleutian Islands of Alaska. The environmental activists in Vancouver were horrified. They feared that apart from releasing radiation, the nuclear weapons might trigger a tsunami in one of the world's most unstable earthquake zones.

The activists had already formed organizations such as Scientific Pollution and Environmental Control society (SPEC). They mounted protest campaigns, using the slogan Don't Make a Wave. The United States went ahead and tested a weapon in October 1969, announcing that this was only the first. Although there was no tsunami, the protests continued and gathered strength.

What's in a name?

In early 1970, as the US planned another nuclear test in the north Pacific, protesters tried a different approach. The Don't Make a Wave Committee, an environmental group in Vancouver, decided to take a boat to the test site to protest on the scene.

At a meeting on 8 February 1970, one of the committee members flashed a two-fingered peace sign (a common gesture at the time). Another member, Bill Darnell, corrected him, saying, 'make that a green peace'.

Darnell's combination of the words 'green' and 'peace' captured the spirit of the era. The colour green – symbolizing growing plants – had become linked to the worldwide environmental movement. Today's political parties tied to the environmental movement still call themselves Greens. Peace was another goal or ideal, which was especially important during that tense cold war period.

Mission statement

Greenpeace's official mission statement describes the organization and its aims in this way: 'Greenpeace is an independent, campaigning organization which uses non-violent, creative confrontation to expose global environmental problems, and to force solutions for a green and peaceful future. Greenpeace's goal is to ensure the ability of the Earth to nurture life in all its diversity.'

Greenpeace operates on the scene, where damaging environmental decisions taken in offices which might be half a world away have an effect. This closeness to the action – and willingness to make sacrifices to get there – gives Greenpeace the edge over other protest groups. But although the organization has devoted supporters around the world, it has limited resources.

The targets of Greenpeace's protests are usually large companies or representatives of national governments or their armed forces, who could crush any other type of direct action. Sometimes the peaceful atmosphere of a protest breaks down, which leads to violence – usually aimed at the Greenpeace representatives. But Greenpeace never plans to use violence in a mission.

Even if it chose to do so, Greenpeace would find it hard to adopt any other strategy to achieve its aims. The peaceful approach does have its advantages. Greenpeace members might be supporters of peaceful protest, but they still know how to use mind bombs (see page 14). Getting the message across so that the wider world hears, sees and reacts, is the key goal of any Greenpeace mission.

WHAT DO YOU THINK?

Turning the other cheek

How do you think a Greenpeace team should react if its members are attacked on a mission – for example, by armed guards working for a logging company in the Amazon rainforest? Can fighting back ever be justified? What would the wider consequences be for Greenpeace in that case?

Closer focus

One reason the Greenpeace Foundation struggled at times was that it lacked focus. The different branches tackled any ecological issue that concerned them: nuclear tests (above and below ground), killing whales or baby seals, air and water pollution, and more.

Sometimes their aims and targets overlapped, which led to more than one organization spending money on a cause that just one branch could have addressed just as well. This lack of direction – and the

Greenpeace activists hang a protest banner at the site of the Greek food importing company Soya Hellas in August 2000. The protesters accuse the company of introducing GM food without properly warning the public.

spending troubles that followed – made the Greenpeace Foundation shaky in 1979. The aim of Greenpeace International since 1979 has been to sharpen its focus. It has narrowed the number of campaigns it undertakes so that it can concentrate on them more closely. This is more like the sort of decision-making that businesses use. It is described as top-down (decisions are made at the highest level and passed down to different branches).

Setting targets

The top-down approach differs from the loosely organized, unfocused approach that was common during the 1970s. But Greenpeace now targets its core issues more closely. The Greenpeace International website identifies the following campaigns:

• Climate
• Forests
• Oceans
• Nuclear issues
• Peace
• GM food
• Toxic chemicals

Below are some of the ways in which Greenpeace runs these campaigns.

Climate

Greenpeace uses its presentation skills to spread information about the dangers of global warming. Its press releases draw attention to heroes and villains in an effort to reduce wasteful – and dangerous – emissions. Greenpeace calls on people to:

• choose to take action;
• study the solutions;
• learn about the science of climate change.

Greenpeace's own efforts, for example, the '2°C makes a big difference to your life' campaign, are hard-hitting and aimed at us all.

A masked Greenpeace protester outside the Agriculture Ministry in Rome, highlights how babies are fed genetically modified soya beans.

Forests

Most people now realize just how important trees are to the health of the planet. Forests are the Earth's lungs, as well as being a vital habitat. More than half the world's plant and animal species inhabit the seven per cent of the world that is covered in rainforest. Greenpeace publicity campaigns and direct action aim to protect this vital natural resource.

Oceans

Greenpeace began operating in the early 1970s by patrolling the waters of the Pacific Ocean off North America. It has kept oceans high on its agenda ever since. Greenpeace confronts companies which pollute the oceans, fishing fleets that threaten precious fish stocks and those who want to carry on whaling when most of the world condemns the practice.

Nuclear issues

Nuclear concerns have remained a constant focus for Greenpeace since the 1970s. Over the years, Greenpeace has protested against undersea tests of nuclear weapons as well as wider issues, such as using nuclear power to generate electricity. Greenpeace is not always negative, however, and adds its voice to those who want sustainable and efficient energy sources.

Peace

World peace (half the Greenpeace name) remains an important concern for the organization. Greenpeace has focused on eliminating nuclear weapons for more than three decades, with a Greenpeace member even dying for this cause (see page 30). At the moment, the world has 30,000 nuclear weapons; about 1500 of these are ready to launch, 24 hours a day.

Genetically modified food

Advances in science have led to many developments in genetic methods which alter plants so that they produce larger harvests or withstand pests more effectively. Some private companies and countries want to introduce such genetically modified (GM) food widely. Greenpeace, like many environmental groups, notes that there is no turning back if these plants breed with existing species. It calls for extreme caution and much more study.

WHAT DO YOU THINK?

Other choices?

Has Greenpeace narrowed its range of campaign issues too much? Can you think of any major environmental topic that is not covered within the issues that Greenpeace addresses? What would Greenpeace be like if it set out to address a wider range of environmental topics, one by one?

Toxic chemicals

Toxic (poisonous) chemicals pollute lakes, rivers, the oceans and the air around us. Greenpeace monitors the scale of damage caused by these chemicals. It is also calling for new partnerships and awareness within industry, so that companies can replace toxic chemicals with less harmful alternatives. Companies listen to Greenpeace, and the results can be dramatic (see 'A Greener Apple', page 38).

A Chinese official snatches an anti-nuclear banner unfurled by Greenpeace activists in the heart of Beijing in 1995.

Direct action

How does Greenpeace put its message across? Are its methods different from those of other international organizations? Today Greenpeace still relies on daring, imagination and courage, just as it did when it began nearly 30 years ago.

These qualities have always been features of a Greenpeace mission. And those involved in the missions might add some more qualities that might not be so obvious to the outside world.

Peace protesters from Greenpeace Germany take their message on to the roof of the Brandenburg Gate in Berlin, once a symbol of German military power.

Timber teamwork

The Forest Stewardship Council (FSC) is an excellent example. In 1990, a number of individuals and organizations – each with an interest in forests and timber – met in California to discuss how the world's forests could be managed sensibly. Those involved included Greenpeace, Friends of the Earth and the World Wide Fund for Nature, all of which urged that forests be preserved. But also represented were IKEA, B&Q, Home Depot and other companies that use forest products.

The FSC grew out of these early discussions, and was founded in 1994. It now sets standards for maintaining forests in a way that still allows companies to harvest timber. The FSC gives its approval to those companies – and privately owned forests – that look to the future by replanting and preserving woodlands. More than 80 million hectares of forest worldwide have passed the strict FSC test. The FSC produces

A Norfolk police officer takes Peter Melchett of Greenpeace into custody after an anti-GM protest in 1999. Melchett and his fellow protesters had destroyed GM crops being studied on a Norfolk farm.

a chain of custody (COC) certificate when it is sure that the wood in a commercial product has been harvested, manufactured and shipped according to FSC standards. People who buy furniture can find this seal on thousands of wood-based products.

Hearts and minds

Greenpeace also recognizes the importance of public opinion. Greenpeace does not have a huge budget for television and newspaper advertisements, but it does find ways of getting its message across to many people.

Greenpeace is one of only three major charities (along with Oxfam and WaterAid) which has an official presence at the Glastonbury Festival. Greenpeace banners and pamphlets encourage music lovers to stop and think about the world environment. And the Greenpeace Field is a popular Glastonbury destination in its own right. Those who arrive hot or muddy can take a shower in water warmed by solar power, or they can lounge on hammocks made from sustainable materials.

Vocal opposition

Greenpeace has made enemies throughout its history. Some opponents are predictable: powerful governments and their armies, large companies which exploit the environment, or whaling vessels.

A few enemies share some of the same basic aims and values as Greenpeace itself. Extreme environmental activists accuse Greenpeace of being too timid. They believe that campaigners should be prepared to break laws for their cause.

Other observers take the opposite view, criticizing Greenpeace when it crosses swords with the law. In July 1999, Greenpeace UK executive-director Peter Melchett and 27 other activists destroyed

GM crops on a 2.6-hectare farm in Norfolk. They were arrested and tried, but found not guilty of trespass and criminal damage.

Not everyone was pleased with this result. Some people argued that an unelected organization (Greenpeace) could do what it liked. And William Brigham, whose farm grew the GM maize, said the legal decision gave 'the green light to trespass and the green light to vandalism… This attack was a frightening experience for myself and my family. Greenpeace is a massive environmental pressure group and we are a small family farm. They used bully boy tactics to get their point across and today the bully has won.'

Kids for Forests

Most young people love to hear about Greenpeace campaigns, whether it is high drama on the high seas, public environmental demonstrations or daring missions to expose the most powerful companies in the world. Greenpeace recognizes this interest, and the important role that young supporters play – not just some time in the future, but here and now.

Kids for Forests is one of the most exciting Greenpeace projects. It offers young people the chance to learn about ancient forests and the threats they face, and more importantly what Greenpeace intends to do to defend these woodlands. The project is aimed at 'children, teens, youth groups, teachers and schools from all over the world'. The first step in joining is to click on the Kids for Forests website.

The website has all sorts of links, for example, to forest maps, galleries of children's drawings and artwork of forests, details of world meetings about ancient forests, and message boards from all around the world.

But the Kids for Forests project is about far more than just informing children. It gives young people the chance to take action in a range of ways. Anyone with real devotion to the cause can become an ancient forest ambassador, spreading the Greenpeace message of conservation across the world.

newspapers, radio and television, the Don't Make a Wave Committee (see page 12) would have been puzzled by some of the ways in which Greenpeace conveys its message today.

During the early 1970s, computers were huge, slow machines, and even experts thought that they were mainly good for number crunching. Since that time, people have bought their own PCs, then hooked up with the Internet, then used laptops with wi-fi connections to communicate with each other. Meanwhile, mobile phones have become widespread, then grown smaller and smaller. Now they even save and transmit images.

Why present this modern history of communications? The answer is simple: Greenpeace has been on the cutting edge of new technology throughout its history. And it has never been easier to learn about – and join in with – Greenpeace campaigns and missions.

The Active Supporters Network

Many people in Britain have their first glimpse of Greenpeace through the Greenpeace Active Supporters Network website. The first paragraph on the home page makes its purpose clear: 'Find out what's happening in your local area, our campaigns, events and training and how you can get involved.'

Greenpeace activities come to life here, with dramatic photographs and on-the-scene accounts which draw people into the life and breath of Greenpeace. And along the way they also find links to specialist sites for Greenpeace UK, as well as wider, international sites such as the Greenpeace Forum.

Greenpeace supporters with a banner and collection tins spread their message at an open-air festival in Edinburgh. Getting people to stop and listen is the first step in building a wider support network.

... ON THE SCENE ... ON THE SCENE ... ON THE SCENE ...

The rolling seas

Although a Greenpeace ship might set sail from port, it does not lose contact with those it leaves behind. Crew members on the Esperanza (see page 27) kept the public in the picture with regular entries on the Greenpeace weblog. They recorded both heroic and routine events, the triumphs and the seasickness, in a way that kept the mission fresh in people's minds. In the entry below, crew member Melanie describes how difficult it is to work while the ship tosses back and forth on the high seas near New Zealand.

'And just as I finished typing that paragraph Captain Frank took the wheel and the ship started rolling more than 30 degrees. My chair slid on the floor all the way to the port side of the ship, but Sara was between me and the wall so the two of us jumbled up in a pile. But just for a moment, because then the ship rolled to port and we slid in a heap into Sakyo at the other end of the office. All the while trying to keep our chairs from flying out from under us, clutching our laptops and trying to prevent notebooks and other office paraphernalia from sliding on to the floor.'

WHAT DO YOU THINK?

Preaching to the converted?

Some people argue that Greenpeace aims its message at those who are its natural allies – young people, festival-goers and other activists – and that it does not try hard enough to win over those who really need convincing. Do you think Greenpeace spends too much time preaching to the converted?

Glossary

civil rights Basic individual freedoms such as freedom of speech and religion and the right to a fair trial.

cold war A period lasting roughly from 1945 to 1991 during which the US and the Soviet Union opposed each other and almost went to war several times.

communist Someone who believes in a system in which all property is owned by the community and each person contributes and receives according to their ability and needs. A communist government provides work, health care, education and housing, but may deny people certain freedoms.

draft dodger Someone who leaves his or her country to avoid being forced (drafted) into military service.

ecology The study of plants and animals within their environment.

emission Waste products discharged from cars, factories and machines.

environment The surroundings or condition in which people, animals and plants live.

expatriate Someone who lives away from his or her native country.

flagship A country's or organization's most important or famous ship.

habitat The place or environment in which a plant or animal normally lives.

hermit Someone who chooses to live alone, away from most other people.

hippie Someone who believes strongly in peace and who rejects many of society's rules about clothing and work.

Industrial Revolution A period beginning in Britain during the 18th century, when new inventions and methods changed the way things were made. Machines did the work of people in many areas.

media The word used to describe the different ways of getting news to the public, including newspapers, magazines, television and radio.

nuclear weapons Destructive weapons that get their power from splitting some of the tiniest particles, such as atoms.

personnel The people who work for or within an organization.

pollution The dirtying of the environment, usually with man-made waste.

radical Someone who supports sudden and extreme change in society.

reserve An area of land set aside to protect wildlife.

resources Natural features such as clean air, timber and water that are used to improve people's lives.

satanic Inspired by or reminding people of the devil.

smog A type of air pollution which is a combination of smoke and fog.

Soviet Union The name given to the country that included Russia and 14 of its neighbours, which united to form a larger communist country from 1917 to 1991.

sustainable Able to be continued without stopping.

terrorism Using violence against innocent people to force governments to agree to demands.

tsunami A high, fast-moving wave caused by an earthquake under the ocean.

Vietnam An Asian country where thousands of American soldiers fought during a fierce war in the 1960s and 1970s.

wi-fi A type of Internet connection that sends a signal to a computer through the air rather than along a wire.

Further reading

Environmental Disaster Alert! P Challen (Crabtree, 2004)

The Greenpeace to Amchitka: An Environmental Odyssey R Hunter (Arsenal Pulp Press, 2005)

Greenpeace (Humanitarian Organizations) A Parry (Chelsea House, 2005)

Greenpeace (Worldwatch) S Sheehan (Hodder Children's, 2003)

Websites

http://archive.greenpeace.org/kidsforforests/about.html
The Kids for Forests site is informative and offers the chance to join one of the most important Greenpeace campaigns.

http://www.greenpeace.org/international/
The main Greenpeace International site offers information on all aspects of Greenpeace, and special kids' pages.

http://www.greenpeaceactive.org.uk/about.php
The Active Supporters Network site shows the depth of support for Greenpeace UK, with tips on how to get involved.

http://weblog.greenpeace.org/
The Greenpeace weblog is constantly updated with news, observations, debates and images.

Index